Hush

Hush

Nicole Lyons

Published in the United States by
Feminine Collective Media

ISBN 9780997962277
Library of Congress Control Number: 2017905311

Editor: Julie Anderson
Cover Design: SA Smith
Typesetting & Layout: SA Smith
Cover Photo: Paul Epson © 2017

For Scott, Brinly, and Tatym.
My nine o'clock summer sunset and our rays of
brilliant light.

Acknowledgements~

I have never been a wealthy woman, have never done anything extraordinary, or accomplished anything remarkable, but I have loved beyond measure, and have been loved remarkably by a few.

It was within that outstanding love, free of judgment and ripe with support, where I found my voice; the one that echoes alongside my mentors, my muses, my friends, and I am forever grateful to each and every one of them. Every day I am in awe of their glorious souls, with voices loud and unashamed of the beauty and the pain they weep onto this world.

My plate is full with the offerings of my tribe, and my table stands proud, forever welcoming the lost souls with hungry mouths and pleasant hearts.

With the deepest gratitude, I acknowledge the ones who have made this collection possible with their endless support and encouragement.

Stephanie Bennett-Henry
Shawna Heaton
Alfa Holden
Dori Owen
Tamara Paul
Lisa Marie Lenna
And to the King of Kings, my brother, Jeremy Tilburt, I am forever awed and grateful that the Universe would give me you.

To my mother, Debbie Peters, the strongest woman I know, without your light, I could never shine on my own. Your sacrifice to be the moral compass and loving beacon has not gone unnoticed. Because of you and your love, there are two North Stars nourished, and ready to guide lost souls like ours, home.

-Nicole Lyons

Little Pieces

How bittersweet
it is to know that
little pieces of my heart
have been scattered
throughout this world
and into the next.
Taken to cities
I will never visit,
sleeping under stars
I will never see,
and waking up
to sleepy love crusted eyes
that will never again
gaze into my own.

Contents

Dropping Leaves of Dreams

A family tree stands,
a great willow.
Rippled branches stretching thick,
reaching the grandest heights
to obscure the sun
and steal the light.

A family tree boasts,
a great willow.
Shooting suckers along hills,
claiming dominance
over pretty paths
long ago deserted.

A family tree sways,
a great willow.
Shooing the crows that perch,
and shading
the birches that dare
grow too close.

A family tree weeps,
a great willow.
Dropping leaves, of dreams
and unhappy children
who would swing
from its branches.

Under the Sycamore

I carved my place in this world,
into the bark of a beautiful
old sycamore tree
long before I cut my teeth
on the boys who would bend
her branches.
My place was crooked
and she was hesitant,
shedding me off in big chunks
quicker than I could pierce her
flesh, but I was forceful,
and she relented.

I was young and untouchable.
Air thinning, mind spinning,
I inhaled freedom
in the muggy summer
sun, and exhaled secrets.
Spewing my soul under a canopy
of hushed greens
and swallows singing.

I hung my hopes
from her branches,
and she, catching sun,
cast stained glass
colours along my pure,
bronzed skin.

I found my peace
on mossy ground,
legs stretched, painted

pink toes tracing
the strong lines of her
supple trunk.
I spent days, like that.
Daydreaming of first kisses
and a love I didn't understand.

I watched her fall.
Reaching tips to dying suns
as she spilled my secrets
into grey skies.
Casting shadows
upon my thirteenth year,
and the dreams she had
dropped at my feet.

I blossomed in the spring,
without her. Alone but for
the gnarled limbs
like burned branches
that carved their place
in this world, into me,
long before I cut my teeth
on the boys who would
never bend my branches.

His place was sacred
and mine. I fought,
ripping chunks of meat
quicker than he could pierce
my flesh, but he was forceful,
and I relented.

She Was

She was reckless
and apprehensive.
She was cruel
and she was kind.
She was a beautiful
contradiction,
living large and
dying inside.

Clusters

It is as if some sort of cosmic energy
is continually pulsing
through my veins,
cascading along, dancing
with my white blood cells, finding
a home in every organ
of my body.
I hold the universe
inside of me,
and I delight
in the idea of that for days
on end,
but when I hit blackest of holes,
the galaxies
that live beneath my skin
never cease.
Bone deep
exhaustion near cripples me,
the melancholy damn near swallows
me alive,
but still, the stars erupt
with every
bump of my heartbeat, and shoot
through my system.
This world is a cruel place
for a mad girl with stars falling
under her skin.

The Darkest Things

Discard your mask
next to me.
For I, too, desire
the darkest things.

Upon Your Arrival

Upon your arrival,
peace departed; cut
the brake lines
and got the hell
out of Dodge, with
my sanity riding shotgun.

How Would You

I have seen love
open souls, how
would you love me?

On my knees, baring
my throat.

Under Red Skies

That night we smoked cigarettes
and talked of the red skies
that hung over us, above
right shoulders just East
of town.

And although it was winter
and chaos danced
with the blowing snow,
I felt the heat
of those red skies.

It was somewhere
inside of forty-five
mile an hour winds
and the second bottle
of wine
where I fell
in love

Sundays and Second Chances

You taste like Sundays
and second chances,
the right turns
when I went left.
And I sure would like
to kiss you some more.

Junk

He was intense,
a drug,
and I couldn't get enough,
no matter how much of him
I consumed.
He was potent and powerful
and he ruined me,
and I yearned to ruin.
I kept going back for more.
I swear if I were to rip
myself open,
it wouldn't be blood
that poured out of me,
it would be him.

Binged & Purged

You would be hard-pressed
to find anything good
in him
but I liked
the way he tasted,
black souled,
beneath my tongue.

Blossom and Bone

I am
blossom and bone
with a soul
on fire,
and I yearn
to touch the steel
of flesh
and icy minds
with hearts willing
to burn.

Desecration

I found the pieces
you tried to hide,
buried in secret
places, untouched.
Oh, how I yearn
to lash the beauty
of them and leave
my stain
upon each one.

Won't You Be Mine?

Cupid lies; splattered
upon my stoop,
wings of ink thrashing
and thundering a goodbye
love on the heels
of a viper's kiss...
won't you be mine,
Valentine...

Dining with Lovers

We drink tears
and eat pain.
Wipe our mouths
and call it
love.

Sticky Sour Dancing

Let us turn on the lights
and take off this skin we are in.
The only thing to come
between our shadows
shall be our bones.
I like the way the light catches
our vulnerability, quivering
in the beds of old fractures.
And the smell of our marrow mixing,
sticky sour dancing under my nose,
wets my tongue, and spills my secrets
through barren valleys, split
between the grooves beneath my hips.

She, of the Darkest

She is of the strangest beauty
and the darkest courage.
and when she walks
with intent
the earth trembles
beneath her feet.

Would You Have Me?

Would you have me
kneel before you,
kissing the unloved places?
My mouth is full, gnawing
on the souls of the restless ones,
who have died on their knees,
before me.

Dancing with Devils

The flames licked
our heathen heels, scorching
flesh long into the night.
The way we moved bled
fevers through seared skin
and cast
the smells of our filth
upon the air,
beckoning the scavengers.
And still, we danced on.

We disturbed the beat
of blackened hearts pounding.
Grinding with the rhythm
of charged pulses, we howled.
The strange tongues thick
in our mouths, provocation
to summon the monster.

Our shadows swung
wildly off
our hips, lunging
into howling mouths
panting for our taste.
We watched
them, the devils
feasting upon each other,
chasing souls into the flames.
The beast smiled. And still,
we danced on.

Gleaming Bones

I would shed my skin
to gleam bones
for you, in every
way you would never
dare ask. And that,
my want to bare
souls while others
skim pretty, is the only
gift I have that is
worthy enough,
to give to you.

They Take Me Under, Sometimes

I have never
seen battles
quite as terrifyingly beautiful
as the ones I fight
when my mind
splinters
and races,
to swallow me
into my own madness,
again.

Neither Heaven nor Hell

He calms my chaos
and I fuel his fire.
We are a match made
between heaven and hell.

The Savage Bits

For him I could
dine on the darkest
things.
Set fireworks
to my soul
and savour the bits
that splatter the walls.

I Will Love You

And I will love you.
In all of the ways
you should have always
been loved, I will love you.

I will dive headfirst into
the depths of your stormy
soul and drop anchors to keep you
from being swept out to sea.

And I will love you.
In all of the ways
you should have always
been loved, I will love you.

I will master the labyrinth
of your brilliant mind
and drop hammers to keep
the walls at bay.

And I will love you.
In all of the ways
you should have always
been loved, I will love you.

I will blow life into
your faded spirit
and drop gold to mend
your broken pieces.

And I will love you.
In all of the ways
you should have always
been loved, I will love you,
until you finally begin
to love yourself, and then
I will love you more.

I Should Have Known Better

He had the smile
of an angel
and the mind
of a devil,
and I should have
known better.
But he planted flowers
in my heart
and made hell
feel like home.

The Offering

I bled out
and into him,
for him, every
time he asked.
And he asked,
and I withered
while I bled
as he watched.

Between Inky Feathers

Perhaps when we kissed,
pieces of my soul found
their way beneath
Death's wing
and became stuck
between inky feathers,
and when she flew
I was so deep
in your eyes
that my stolen soul
was not missed
until you dropped
your kiss
from my mouth,
and the emptiness in me
became thick, and ached
until I took it to darker places.

When My Shadow Speaks

You demand my pretty
words on happy days
to mend your broken heart,
but when the sun hits my back
and my shadow speaks
its truth, you cower
in horrified judgment.
You say you want
to know my soul
but the truth is that
my light would blind you
long before you could ever
drown in my darkness.

Shades of Never Enough

I bleed truth
and trying
to please you,
but all you see
are the shades
of never enough,
dripping from the pen
that you gave to me.

But You Were

Not all prisons
have locks
not all secrets
are sacred
but you
were
midnight whispers
trapped inside
twisted minds
and heavy hearts

Gambling With Souls

Some of us sell pretty
versions of our ugly
selves and call it truth;
others fold our pretty
truths into ugly lies
and call it even.
We are illusionists,
realists, the gamblers
of souls, and we all pay
the poet, in the end.

Godless

I manifested him.
Somewhere between
my dreams
and nightmares,
I gave him life.

Nocturnal Places

He lit my world up
and left me
stumbling
through darkness.
Find me
in nocturnal places,
feeding loneliness
into hungry mouths.

Beneath Darkness

We were not made
of star stuff.
Perhaps the ash
ground beneath
Lucifer's boot
is where we
were born.

On a Kiss

On a kiss, life slipped
passed devastated lips
and faded into lungs of sorrow.
And I have lived breathless ever since,
choking on the urge to exhale
and be free to find you again.
But if I slip
and breathe you into their grieving eyes
I will see you dancing
upon their sympathies
before they blink,
and your curtain is drawn again.
So I shall inhale,
and hold you,
bursting in my heart,
burning against the walls of my lungs
until the day your kiss slips
from my lips again,
and carries our last breath away
together.

Unhinged and Half-Starved

He was wildfire,
and I wanted to burn.
I loved his fury,
the way he left me
half-starved and crazy,
dangling over the edge
of obsession to see
how far I would fall

A Furious Ascension

She watched stiff-backed
girls in snow-white paper
dresses flying,
their speckled kites
low to the ground,
and she called
for the great gusts
of angry winds
to blow in and catch
the corners
of those dresses
and kites,
and take them
all, tangled together
into stormy places
behind her eyes.
Sweep them
into deep places
where held breath burns
against walls of lungs
before sighing
into ecstasy.

Leave them
in dark places
where terrified screams burn
the backs of throats,
and rip pain
into pleasure.
Bury them
among stark bones
that found their lustre
in the depths
of her mind.

I Could Almost Sparkle

The truth is I liked the filth of it all.
I was a fucking mess,
but eventually life demanded
cleanliness, and eventually
I could almost sparkle.
Still every now and again I'll slip,
and cast my shadow to the delight
of the other sparkling messes
afraid of their own.
They cool their heels
and laugh, patting each other
on the backs for shining
so bright that their tiny things
will grow dull. I watch them
from my shadow, wrapped
in the warmth of my cleanest
tiny things that will grow wild
and bright despite the mess of me,
and in that moment,
when their lights fade
and the breeze meets the sweat
on the back of my neck,
in that moment I am clean.

The Ties That Bind

They speak of blood
as if it was a sacred tie
that binds me to the fools
who have twisted
my words into the noose
around my neck.
But the knot is weak,
tied with oily fingers
attached to hands
upon hands casting stones
at my feet.
And I have spent a lifetime
looking upon their glass houses
while I untangled myself
from their ties, and now
they are nothing more
than ink, smudged,
between these pages.

Stealing Breath

There are lost souls
wandering,
stealing breath
to be the ones,
who breathe
life back in.
And sometimes,
I find myself
walking among them.

In All That I Am

If I could draw a blade across my wrist
to show you that my veins clog
with the sludge of ugliness, you would
never again ask me,
"Why are you so tired?"
If I could crack open my skull
to free my mind, you would
see that it is not splintered
by madness but rather patched
together with clarity, you would
never again ask me
to swallow poison.
If I could rip this body open
to show you the raw red wounds
that have been lashed onto my soul
by every inhumane atrocity
this world has endured, you would
never again ask me,
"Why are you so sad?"
Instead, your accusing eyes demand
simple words to simpler questions that
the simplest minds can process.
And in all that I am,
simple I am not.

Distorted

I stand here in gilded glory,
and I watch you,
while you're looking
into me – horrified.
I see you,
every last inch of you.
I watch you waste your time
wasting away,
so I serve you.
I feed your vile words back
into your hungry mouth,
and I stare – transfixed.
I see you,
savour the taste
I watch as you suck
on your self-hatred.
Your dull eyes
finally light up,
your cheeks flush
as you gag back your loathing.
I see you,
while you stand before me,
barely skimming the surface.
I watch you walk away, turning
your back to me
before I can show you
what everyone else sees
when they see you.

Evanescence

I swear I was clean
before you came blazing in,
guns firing hot, bursting into me
with pain so sweet
that I begged for a slow death.
But you stole the sweet
ache from my bones
and left the savage bits
of you behind, spraying them
all over my world.
They blot out the sun,
and leave me with a forever night.
They crawl over me, inside of me,
and consume me
with the filth of memories.
And they whisper
about this slow death
and how I should be careful
what I wish for.

Little Deaths

There are little deaths
in every bit
of remembering,
and all of
the forgetting.
The truth is
I don't know
if I should
bleed for you,
or for me.

The Night A Blue Moon Burst

The sun has set a thousand times
since the night a blue moon burst
and I opened my door to a wolf
grinning wildly, chewing on my name.
My, what spectacular eyes he had;
deep pools of golden madness
churning the reflection of my surprise
into blazing fire that broke his gaze
and seared fear into my flesh.
My pulse raced, leaping to ride
the sweet stench of terror ripping
holes through my veins before it danced
under the great weight of his paws
crushing the walls of my chest.
The sun has set a thousand times
since the night a blue moon burst,
and cast its shadow upon pebbles,
and the wolf that would steal my breath.
But even now, on the eve of a rising
I can barely breathe until I hear them
howling in the distance,
and then I will drift,
pulling wilderness from my hair
under the light of a quiet moon.

Crushed, Wet Wildflowers

She tasted like
wildflowers; crushed,
wet wildflowers carried
in sticky palms
through farmers' fields,
just before dawn.

Discharged

It was addicting,
the attempt
to lose myself
inside of all
the others, until
I chilled my bones
in the shadows
cast by stoic
backs and upturned
eyes that refused
to see me, sacrificing.
There is no colder poetry
than that of the tragedies
of found girls, aching
to become lost.

Steady

Remember when you were a child
and you would throw your arms out
and spin wildly in circles?
If you didn't set your eyes on one spot,
focus on a steady, the spinning would
become too much, and you would tumble
sick to the ground.
My mind gets like that sometimes too
with its terrible racing and raging,
and it always becomes too much,
and I tumble sick to the ground.
But with my mind it is so much harder
to catch my breath. I can't lie there
like I could when I was a child,
on the ground, waiting on my balance
with the sun warming my cheeks.
No, when my mind tumbles me to the ground,
I am sick for a long time.
It takes much more than the sun
to pick me back up again.

But now I know. I have finally, after all this time
figured it out. I just have to focus my eyes,
just one little thought, and hold on to a steady,
and you, My Love, are my steady.
You have always been that steady,
and had I just stopped spinning for a moment,
I would have caught you out of the corner of my eye,
waving and running to catch me
every single time before I tumbled.

About a Reaper's Kiss

Had death
not kissed you
sweeter
than I ever had,
hell would never
look so good.

The Colour of Us

Water is wet and grass is green
and we are us, until it isn't
and we aren't, anymore.
And that's how it was, he and I,
right from the start: peas and carrots,
sand and surf, heaven and hell.
We were the late night phone calls
that went straight to voicemail,
the last light in the window
when all other doors were locked.
We were voracious laughter
muffling horrified screams.
We were bodies twisted in ecstasy
and minds broken in angst.
We were psych stays and breakdowns,
pills popped and death threats,
sirens wailing and holding cells.
We were life, on a September morning,
and death on an April night.
And in our own minds we were golden.

Tasting Pain

I loved him – intensely.
Throat bared, holes in the walls,
sirens wailing – intensely.

But God, did I love him.
I knew we would end
before we had even begun.
But my name was blackened
on his chest and
confessions had been whispered
at three am and
I couldn't breathe without him.

And until you have
tasted pain as sweet as his,
you can't begin to understand.

The Unraveling

Oh, how I loved
the unraveling,
of hearts
and promises.
I met my beauty
in the pain
when your truth
hit the floor.

Hiding Beauty

I am told there is beauty in pain.
Maybe beauty is hidden
in the blood that stains
dirty floors, leaking
from the tips of fingers
that curl, and claw
the way to doors,
broken and unhinged.
Perhaps beauty swirls
in the bowl,
mingling with bile
retched out in shame.
Does beauty lurk
in the shadows, creeping
over naked bodies writhing
on the floor, gasping
for breath that betrayal
has cut off?
I am told there is beauty in pain,
but I wonder
if beauty sleeps in the eyes
of those who turn their backs
and thank God
it isn't theirs.

Amnesia

Just for tonight
let's forget to remember
how we hurled our words,
like bottles filled with hate
smashing against the walls
of each other's hearts,
and how we delighted
in the little cuts we made.
Just for tonight
let's forget to remember
how we poked those little cuts,
grinding filth in deep,
and how we numbed ourselves
to the taste of our shame.
Just for tonight
let's forget to remember
how we let our sick hearts die,
and how we watched shadows swirl
and take us both under.
Just for tonight
let's remember how we
once loved so intensely that together
we could drive light
into the darkest of places.

Let Old Bones Lie

I never could tell
if it was my body
or my mind
he ached to strip.

He had a weakness
for pretty disasters
and ugly tragedies.
The cut
of his tongue
sliced through both.

Colors exploded
into me, violent
shades of him,
striking my soul.

Hush
your quaking
heart,
we have many
things to see.

Calling
rings hollow now
on the heels
of those
violent bells.

Let old bones
lie, I will
cut you
fresh roses.

Draw the cold
from my bones
and break me,
again. He was
the sweetest
regret I ever had
to swallow.

After Last Call

We shall rejoice
and sit pretty
on forsaken thrones
emblazoned
with dirty verses
and guarded
by inky wings.

Eerie Alones and Jams of Traffic

It's an eerie kind of alone
when your world comes crashing down
and you're on your knees
with nothing but agony
for company.
When everything is spinning
out of control
and you are powerless
to get back what is gone,
clarity hits hard.
How strange it is, when a life shatters.
The sun still rises; traffic still jams
and people carry on.
It's an odd feeling
to scream into nothing
and ask for a pause
just for one second,
to catch a breath.
Because life should stop
for a moment,
at that moment
when your world has fallen apart,
just so you can catch
your breath. It's a long road,
and when we walk
with pain we walk alone.

Lilacs on Leaving

I look for you,
still. Reaching
through sound waves,
blaring, to pluck you
from nothing
back into existence.
I wait for you,
still. Walking
blurry lines of almost
there and crossing too
far gone.
I smell you,
still. Scraping
lilacs down metal
along shortcuts to easy.
Prying life
out of the jaws
of a crash,
you used
to call home.

A Quiet Hum

Why does this world
not rise up to meet
the slamming
of my heart breaking
against its cage?
Surely it is not
a quiet hum. Or perhaps
the breaking is what
became the beating
long ago.

Hunger Pains

We starved ourselves
of sleep, but we gorged
on each other, and every
other thing they had
warned us about.
It was glorious,
and enlightening, and
tragic, and every now
and then I refuse my meals
and reminisce about the days
when I went hungry,
and filled myself on the
decadence they tried to keep
for themselves.

Summer Sunset

You are my nine o'clock
summer sunset.
The scent of honeysuckle
and sweet pea breezing
through the bones of trees
and in through my open window.

Fade Out

There was a moment
when the neon
caught the silver
that I thought to myself,
This is going to make a wicked mess.

But the lights
went down
and everything
faded to black.

Soul Screamer

I hear them sometimes
when the moon is full.
She pulls the cries
from their throats
and places them in
the waves that break
against the shore.
And they ripple through
me when she is new
before madness sweeps
them back out to sea
and I howl again.

Sit Pretty

I want to be cruel.
I want to lash out at everyone
who has used me,
and I want to do it over
and over again.
I want them all to know
what ungrateful feels like.
I want them
to wear the cloak of unloved,
slip into taken for granted,
and sit pretty in thankless.
I want them to feel
what it is like to be sliced
open so the vampires can feed.
I want them to give and give
and give until they have nothing
left to give, and then
I want them to give some more.
And then maybe, just maybe
they will understand.

The Good Kill

I have dug trenches in
the deepest corners
of my mind
to capture, and keep
you, locked, inside
my forgotten playground.
But you storm the chain
link and surge
through razor wire
onto the rapid-fire
battleground of my regrets
and raging thoughts.
Legs coiled
ready to strike,
I see you war-weary,
ready to retreat
into ditches,
opening fire and turning
trenches into graves.

Regret

Regret.
My wistful
lost lover
has returned
to torment me.
Churning riptides
through my veins
to breach my heartbreak,
and flood his madness into my soul.

Rattling on Passed

The ghosts of my past
are stirring within the ruins
of my soul.
I hear them rattling
their chains of regret
to the beat of my name
on their lips.

Are the ghosts
of your past rattling
your chains, again?
Or are you
just missing
and reminiscing
and rattling theirs?

Just Deserts

If only you would vanish
and stay
hidden away in some desolate place,
buried and long forgotten,
I wouldn't feel this need
to escape
my own mind
and the memories that lurk within.
They enthral me
in the sickest way,
these thoughts upon memories
born out of the torment
you fed me.
And sometimes the taste of them,
the regret,
surges back into my mouth,
thick like honey,
to stick to my tongue.
And I would be lying
if I told you
that I didn't think
about going back
for a second helping

Meet Me At The Weeds

I'm almost certain
I'm not going to find you
at the bottom of a bottle,
but tonight the cellars
are stocked and the bartender
is pouring for free.

Sinister Lovers

I have come
to believe that death
and insomnia
are the most sinister lovers
For it is only
at three a.m.
when I am restless
that my body aches
with phantom pains
and your ghost returns
to torment my mind.

Gluttony

My memories of you
are bittersweet now,
like the punch
of green apples
hitting the back
of my tongue.
I gnash my teeth
against their bite
and tear them open
until the sweet
syrup of you
drips down my throat,
and I swallow
what used to be us.

Burned Out

We're burning
among dying stars,
fading out
of their enlightenment.

Perhaps I Will Eclipse

Inside of whispers
and hazy faces
I had lost myself
again, and I called
out to the sun
to find me, reaching
dying arms toward
her fading light
before I turned,
and marked my grave
in the blue warmth
of the moonlight's glow.

Peace by Piece

It's during the moments when I'm quiet
that I foolishly give in to the idea
of peace.
I should know better
by now.
With every blow you laid
on me, you stripped me
of any chance
of peace
that I could have hoped for.
Now the bruises
have healed,
the scars blended
into shades
of me,
faded into almost
gone...almost.
The almost is what kills me
again,
taunts me and tells me what a coward I was.
It's the almost,
the faded pieces
that bring
up everything I never did,
every single thing
I never said.

Unspoken fears rise up
and curdle
against my tongue.
They threaten
to choke me.
So I swallow them,
again,
every last word
I never said to you,
and the burn
explodes through my body,
shredding it
piece by piece,
promising a life
without peace,
if they go unsaid
once more.

Soul Puller

Perhaps she is not
of this world;
the way she slips
into the abyss
with never a need
to come back
up for air, only urges
to reach into the souls
of her kind, and pull
them under too.

Depression Sleeps

Tonight I will sleep.
I will sleep away
the sadness,
and when I wake
I hope to find
that I did not sleep
my entire life away.

Tasting Shame

When the madness spews
from my lips, it's your
shame that breaks me.
As if kissing my darkness
wasn't what hooked you
from the start.

Hush

If I could claw
the words out of
the back
of my throat and give them,
dripping of me, to you,
we would talk of sticky hands,
and the messes they make.

Mind Fuck

Perhaps it wasn't
only my hair
he had knotted
in his fist;
for upon my release
I found my mind
had been pulled
as if it had knees
on which I would beg
as I crawled toward him,
neck deep in a pool
of silver and my name;
reaching to cling
to the tip
of his forked tongue.

In The Absence of Melancholy

Fear no longer sits with melancholy;
it dances wildly, trumpeting its arrival
upon the departure of sadness.
There was security in despair,
as if depression was some sort
of cloak of invisibility, and wrapping
myself in it ensured my quiet
observation of the world.
Fear has stripped me of my cloak
to parade me naked
through rush hour traffic,
an amusing distraction
for the hordes of unforgiving eyes.
The echoes of laughter
have found a way deep into
the canals of my ears, riding
the waves into my brain to stick
like terrible songs; melodies
that pine for lost loves
like melancholy and me.

The Value of a Beautiful Heart

Even after
they scattered
her secrets to the wind
she still loved fiercely,
because she knew
one day someone
would come across
her discarded dreams
and hold them close
enough to believe
in love again.
She never
guarded her heart
because she knew its value
and she gave it to those
who needed it most,
the ones who would
destroy it. And that
is what made her exquisite.

Longing

Longing.
My most shameless
of lost lovers
has returned
to cross the oceans
of my eyes and stake
temptation as his claim.

Between Breakfast and Bedsheets

Even now at the end
of my summer
I look for one.
Skin just so
and weathered
from the sun,
swinging defiantly
from the branches
overlooked.
I pluck it, and
the weight is good
in my palm.
My thumb
makes quick work
of swirling
down the valley
to warm the flesh
before burying my face
into hot fuzz.

And it gives
way between my teeth,
creamy texture
dropping its dress
beneath my tongue
dripping down
my face and elbows
as if it were me,
plucked
seasons too soon,
caught
between breakfast
and bedsheets.

The Bone Keeper

I have cleaned my closet
of all of the bones
to make room
for wispy summer dresses.
I wrapped those bones
in shame
and tucked them deep
into bags of guilt.
With the strings of regret
I tied the bags closed
and knotted them
with resentment.
I lifted the bags
one by one,
the weight of their bitterness
trying to crush me,
and I carried them
to the spot
where the bend finally breaks.

I dug deep to pull strength
to shred earth.
And I dug.
Passed coffins and fossils
I didn't stop until I hit
never again.
My twisted arms
were mighty
when I pulled myself out
of that pit.
And as I stood
I exhaled gratitude
and let the bags fall
into the abyss,
no longer the keeper
of your bones.

I Have Fallen

I have fallen hard,
swirled to the bottom
of a bottle of Jack, stuck
to the blade after
the perfect line was cut.
I have had life breathed
back into me, great
thrusts upon my heart
cracking ribs, as if pain
could will me to stay.
I walked the halls
of the damned, kissed
death herself and told her,
'not quite yet.' I have
swallowed poison
to placate others,
and switch myself off.
I have died
one hundred deaths
to appease doctors,
and family, and friends,
and I did it all
in the name of sanity.

I found myself one
thousand miles from home
in the arms of strangers,
The Enlightened;
and because of them,
their nourishment, I have
accepted my torment. I have
breathed in my darkness
and welcomed it home,
surrendered to the beauty
that was my undoing,
and in acceptance I found
the exquisite jewel that I am.

O Negative

She was beautiful; all thorns
and no roses, but he didn't
mind bleeding.

Stripped

I wear you,
still.
Your scent
covers me
like dirty
clothes
I can't wait
to peel off,
and kick
to the floor.

The Silence of You

Even now,
when the wind
whispers your name
across my skin,
the silence of you
is deafening.

Tomb Gazing

Every now
and then
I roam
the catacombs
in my head
and attempt
to resurrect you,
and make you
shiny again.

Percussion

I never meant
to ruin him,
but I do love
the way his heart
still beats
my name.

Pocket Change

She was brilliance, a rare currency
the entitled would use, but
like all coins, eventually her
value decreased. She became tarnished
from years of being shoved deep
inside pockets, spent in order to fix
problems and save days. Toned up.
Brilliant colours flashed in the sun,
dropping bait while the sharks
gambled her worth. She spun,
flipped, twisted, and twirled high
in the air. Heads you own,
tails you're owned, and discarded,
a slipped tip on a slow night.

After, You

There is peace
within me.
Patiently waiting
for the chaos
to sleep.

A Slow Leak

Little
by little,
drop
by drop,
everything
fades away.

The Long Road Home

It's been awhile since I've walked
this dusty road,
but I remember it well.
That spot there,
where the sun never quite reaches,
is where I found myself
on my knees
praying to a God
I didn't believe in.
Bodies upon bottles
upon razor blades gleaming
with self-harm and a cocaine glow
fill the ditches beside me,
and the trenches of my memories.
In this place the hills are alive
with the sound of sudden drops
and last gasps,
and the air is thick
with the stench of shame.
This is a long road,
and east is west
and north is every failure
I have ever eaten.
South lies,
between humility
and every lie I have ever
sworn in blood.

That Day, At Dinner

The day she chose to strip herself
of everyone else's opinions
was the first time she knew strength,
held courage, and felt beauty.
That was the day when she finally understood
what it meant to be free.

From Steady Shores

Oh my darling, you have eaten
far too many shadows to ever
believe that you have
spent even one day hiding.
A lighthouse can never see
the brilliance of its own light
guiding lost souls home.
It stands tall in the darkness,
steady, a beacon
for the hands that reach
and pull bodies to safety.
You are a lighthouse.
And they do push you
down to pull themselves
up, but you are steel
and blossom and bone,
and when lighting does strike,
the burst of your own radiance
will be so great that you
will finally understand
your own thunder.

Can't Have it All

I need you
to look me in the eyes
and go to battle
with the demons
that lurk
and look back
at you, and then
I need you
to love us back
into redemption.

I See You

I see you.
I see you grinding
another day, battered
and exhausted
refusing to stop.
I see your fists,
swollen and split
knuckled; dripping
with the quit
you beat to the ground.
I see you,
your tired eyes,
bloodshot from blinking
against the grains
of you'll never be enough,
swirling sandstorms
across your vision.
I see you,
beat down
and getting back up.

I see you,
the fight in you,
and it is ferocious.
I see you,
the heart of you,
and it is breathtaking.
I see you,
the soul of you,
and it is magnificent.
I see you,
all of you,
and you are fucking beautiful.

The Cosmos Are In a Goddess

She has stars
in her eyes
and poetry
on her lips,
and loving a girl
like her
will bring you
to your knees.

Someday, Someone

I hope
that someday
when I am gone,
someone,
somewhere,
picks my soul up
off of these pages
and thinks,
"I would have loved her."

About the Author:

Nicole Lyons is a force of nature disguised as a writer, a social activist, a voice for the downtrodden, and a powerful poet with a delicate touch. She lives a good life in beautiful British Columbia with her brilliant daughters and gorgeous husband. In her free time, Nicole volunteers as a speaker and event coordinator with a Canadian non-profit that focuses on suicide awareness and prevention.

Website: thelithiumchronicles.org
Facebook: facebook.com/nicolelyonspoetry
Twitter: @LithChronicles
Instagram: @nicolelyonspoetry

27010040R00072

Printed in Great Britain
by Amazon